Animals That Make Me Say OUCH!

NATIONAL WILDLIFE FEDERATION

Animals

NATIONAL
WILDLIFE
FEDERATION®

That Make Me Say

OUCH!

Dawn Cusick

imagine!
Publishing

Image copyrights held by the photographers on page 79

An Imagine Book
Published by Charlesbridge
85 Main Street
Watertown, MA 02472
(617) 926-0329
www.charlesbridge.com

Library of Congress Cataloging-in-Publication Data
is available upon request.

ISBN: 978-1-62354-042-5

Printed in China. Manufactured in June, 2014.

(hc) 10 9 8 7 6 5 4 3 2 1

Display type and text type set in Motter Corpus and Frutiger.

Jacket and Type Design: Megan Kirby
Proofreading: Brett Blofield
Produced by EarlyLight Books

For information about custom editions, special sales,
premium and corporate purchases, please contact
Charlesbridge Publishing at specialsales@charlesbridge.com

Contents

Introduction

Welcome to a world that will make you say OUCH!

We share Earth with millions of animals. In most places, there is not enough food and habitat to go around, and animals use some amazing adaptations in their bodies and behaviors to help them compete.

Swans and other cold-weather animals, for example, use snow blankets to stay warm. Large wild cats such as lions and tigers use sharp canine teeth to cut off the air supply of prey, and some clownfish secrete special mucus that protects them from sea anemone stings.

On your mark . . . get set . . . say OUCH!

Foraging OUCH!

FORAGING: the act of searching for food

From leaps to stings, animal foraging can make you say OUCH! Animals use behavior tricks and anatomy adaptations to help them find food.

Run for Your Life!

It may look like the zebra in this photo is about to become the lion's dinner. According to the photographer, the zebra escaped after it gave the lion a strong kick! Lion research has shown that when lions hunt alone, they catch prey about 15% of the time. When lions hunt in groups, they are twice as likely to catch prey, but then they have to share their food. Which way would you hunt if you were a lion: alone or in a group?

Eating with Your Mouth Full?

Hundreds of tiny tube feet may help sea stars move fast, but they are no match for a sea gull's strong beak. Sometimes gulls eat sea stars in one bite; other times, gulls shake sea stars until they break into small pieces.

Snake Snacks

People spend a lot of time talking about how snakes get large prey foods through their mouths. It may be more interesting, though, to talk about how snakes get large food down their esophagus. The esophagus is a narrow tube that connects the mouth to the stomach. Luckily for snakes (and unluckily for the prey they eat), the esophagus tube is very stretchy in carnivores that eat large, moving prey.

Hunting Strategies

The ways animals hunt and kill their prey may seem odd or silly when you first learn about them, but usually there are good reasons. Carnivores such as foxes that feed on many types of animals have many different strategies. Prey animals are usually better at avoiding predators because they have more to lose: prey animals can lose their lives, while predators only lose a meal.

Mouse Leaps

When foxes find mice, rats, and other small mammals with their excellent senses of hearing and smell, they leap up and out, landing on top of the rodent and pinning their prey. Hunting this way shortens the amount of time their prey has to escape. Young foxes learn to "mouse leap" from their parents, and they usually lose many meals as they learn. Foxes also eat plants, fruits, fungi, insects, earthworms, small reptiles, birds, marsupials, and other mammals. Coyotes (above) are in the same family as foxes, and they also use mouse leaps to hunt for rodents.

fox

Foraging OUCH!

Tiger Teeth

A tiger's teeth are an important part of its hunting strategy. When killing large animals, tigers suffocate their prey by biting through their tracheas, which cuts off their air supply. When killing small animals, tigers bite through the prey's neck vertebrae with their sharp canine teeth, which breaks their preys' spinal cord so they cannot move. Surprisingly, tigers are only successful at catching prey five to ten percent of the time.

Sensational Cells

When we look at large carnivores such as lions, tigers, and bears, we often see them as fierce because of their large teeth and sharp claws. Surprisingly, a carnivore's best hunting trait may be its nerve cells. These special cells, called neurons, bring information to and from the brain.

This fierce-looking lion uses hundreds of neurons at the base of each whisker to collect information about air movements. These changes in air pressure tell lions which directions prey and predators are coming from, and help them avoid walking into rocks or trees when it's dark.

Sharp Nails

Look at your fingernails for a minute. How short are they compared to the length of your fingers? The claws on brown bears are made from the same type of protein, keratin, as your fingernails, but their nails are as long or longer than your fingers! Brown bears use their long, sharp nails to dig dens and to dig up roots and seeds for food. When hunting for food, bears use the large, flat surface of their front paws to strike their prey.

Foraging OUCH!

Jaws & Claws

Wolverines cause confusion in some people. Their common names are skunk bear and devil bear, but they are not bears. Wolverines are the largest members of the weasel family, and their relatives include otters, badgers, ferrets, and martens. Their strong sense of smell helps them find prey, and their sharp claws help them quickly dig long tunnels down to hibernating animals or dead animals covered in snow. People have seen wolverines fighting bears and wolves to defend their catches.

Free Rides

Many mammal moms move their young from one place to another in their jaws, gently biting down on the loose skin on their offspring's necks. This loose skin is called the scruff. Being inside a lion's mouth may look painful — OUCH! — but since the scruff area does not have many nerve endings, riding in mom's mouth does not hurt. Cubs do not struggle or try to get away when they are in mom's mouth.

Foraging OUCH!

coyotes

Patient Teachers

Mammal moms such as the coyote, cheetah, and tiger spend a lot of time with their young, and feed them with milk. In between feedings, cubs and pups often bite and climb on their moms and their siblings. These behaviors may look like play, but they are important ways for young animals to develop their muscles and learn simple fighting skills.

Don't Move!

Parents put their paws down when they get tired of cub play.

cheetahs

tigers

Think about It . . .

Open your mouth in front of a mirror and look at your upper and lower jaws. Suppose your upper jaw were twice as long as your lower jaw, like a marlin's jaw? What would you look like? And how would you eat an ice cream cone?

Foraging **OUCH!**

Hunting Style

The striped marlin's long, thin upper jaw helps it feed on large fish, crabs, mantis shrimp, and jumbo flying squid. When marlins feed on large groups of schooling fish, their spear-like bill helps them stun and kill many fish at the same time. Marlins often hunt in the same places as dolphins. They wait for the dolphins to herd a fish school into a tight group called a bait ball, then the marlins swim into the ball and steal some of the dolphins' catch!

Olympic Divers

Blue-footed boobies are well known for their blue feet, cool courtship dance, and funny-sounding name. Boobies often hunt for fish in large groups, flying downward from heights of 60 feet at speeds of up to 60 miles per hour. Like other birds that forage this way, they have some cool adaptations that help them. Their skulls, for instance, have areas filled with air that protect their brains from the force of impact.

Bite Protection

Birds are well suited to feeding on snakes. Their beaks, feathers, and scales offer some protection from bites. Herons and owls kill their snake prey by squeezing down with their beaks to cut off the snake's air supply. Other birds kill snakes by dropping or kicking them.

Foraging OUCH!

Head First

When birds such as eagles and this cormorant catch large fish, they often toss them in the air and swallow them head first. Are the birds entertaining themselves by playing with their food before eating it? Nope. Birds know that the spines of many large fish go in one direction. These spines are sharp enough to stick in their throats if they eat the fish tail first.

Snake Sushi

This burrowing owl needs to eat its fresh-caught food quickly to prevent a larger bird from swooping in and stealing it.

Dive for Your Dinner

Cormorants search for food along the sandy bottoms of lakes and oceans. Under water, they hunt for fish, shrimp, crayfish, mussels, snails, and insect larvae. On land, they search for frogs and small reptiles.

Hey, wait a minute . . . How can cormorants find food under water? Like fish, reptiles, and many marine and dessert mammals, they have a protective third eyelid called the nictitating membrane. This membrane works like goggles to protect their eyes under water.

Cormorants do not have the same protective oils in their feathers as other aquatic birds do. These oils waterproof the feathers, allowing the birds to swim in and dive under water without getting their feathers wet. Instead, cormorants hold their wings open when they leave the water so their feathers can dry in the sun's heat.

Diving for Dinner

Common kingfishers live in Africa, Europe, and Asia. Although they often look like large birds in photographs, they measure only about 6.5 inches from one end of their body to the other. Long, sharp beaks help kingfishers hold fish that are fighting for their lives. Kingfishers also use their beaks when they are competing with other kingfishers for the same fishing territories. When fighting, kingfishers grab the other bird's beak and try to push the bird underwater.

eagle

Storytelling Beaks

Bird beaks vary in shape from species to species. Beaks are formed from keratin layered over jawbones. These thick layers of keratin are strong, but flexible. (Keratin is the same protein your fingernails are made from.) Birds do not have teeth, so their beaks often serve the role of teeth, too. The shape of a bird's beak tells you a lot about the type of food it eats. Eagles and other vultures use a large, sharp hook on the tip of their upper beak to tear the flesh of their prey.

Foraging OUCH!

Pollinating Beaks

Hummingbirds have long, thin, pointed beaks. These beaks don't make people or animals say OUCH. Instead, they help the birds get to nectar that other animals cannot reach, and pollinate the flowers they feed from.

Seed-Eating Beaks

Compare the hook in this parrot's beak to the hook in the eagle's beak. Parrots have more room between their upper and lower beaks. They use this extra space to crush strong seeds.

Mature for Their Age

The American avocet uses its long, curved beak to find small insects, crabs, and other invertebrates in shallow marsh water and mud. Unlike most birds, avocets hatch with their eyes open and have warm down feathers to keep them warm. Hatchlings stay with their parents for protection from predators and to learn how to forage for food. Parents use their long beaks to herd hatchlings to safety and to guide them to good feeding sites.

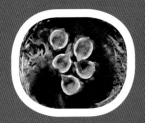

Foraging OUCH!

Orange Marks the Spot!

Female hummingbirds feed their young a mixture of insects and nectar. This partially digested mixture is regurgitated (vomited) from the mother's crop. The bright colors inside the young birds' mouths remind their parents to feed them.

Joke of the Day

How does a young common loon bird take a fresh-caught sunfish from its mother's beak? Very carefully!

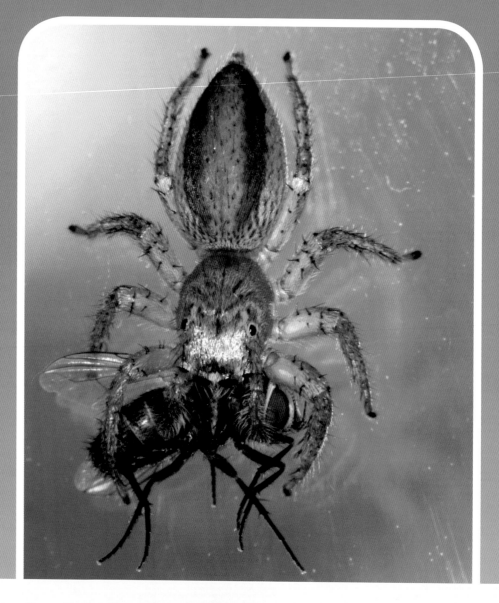

Looks Can Be Deceiving

Spiders may look like they are eating their prey one bite at a time, the way we might eat a slice of watermelon. They actually feed very differently than people. Larger spiders first crush their prey, then vomit up digestive enzymes to break the prey down into a soupy liquid that they can suck up. Smaller spiders vomit their digestive enzymes into fang holes they make in their prey.

Foraging OUCH!

Sharp Spines

Praying mantises are ambush predators with excellent vision. They sit quietly and wait for prey to come by, often camouflaging well with foliage or flowers. Lined with sharp spines, a mantid's large forelegs catch prey and hold it during feeding.

Movable Feasts

Many hornworm caterpillars serve as all-you-can-eat buffets for wasp larvae. Some female wasps lay their eggs in the caterpillars. When the eggs hatch, the larvae feast on the caterpillars. In this photo, you can see wasp pupae in their white cocoons.

Deceiving Looks

Cuckoo wasps often receive oohs and ahhs for their sparkly blue and green exoskeleton colors. They earned their common name for a behavior they share with cuckoo birds called brood parasitism. Instead of laying eggs in their own nests, both cuckoo birds and cuckoo wasps lay their eggs in another animal's nest. The wasp larvae feast on the host insect's larvae or on dead spiders and insects that the host insect left for her own larvae to eat.

Foraging OUCH!

Chemical Calls

Caterpillars have a bad reputation with gardeners and farmers for eating lots of leaves. Plants may seem defenseless — they do not have feet to run or teeth to bite or fins to swim or wings to fly. However, biologists have found that caterpillar saliva cause some plants to release chemicals that attract the caterpillars' predators. The predators get a free meal, and the plant gets relief from the caterpillar feeding!

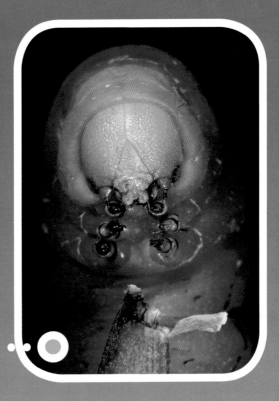

Feeding Ground

Ants spend a lot of time on plants, but they do not eat leaves. They often find foods such as snail slime and vomit, fruits, and plant-eating insects on leaves.

BIG NUMBERS

There are more than 900,000 known species of insects in the world, and more than 80 percent of the world's species are insects. These may sound like large numbers, but biologists believe there are millions more species that have not been discovered yet.

Fierce Faces

Red wasps may look fierce, but their mouth parts are adapted for chewing caterpillars and small insects, not biting large mammals like us. Farmers are glad to see red wasps in their fields because the wasps feed on caterpillars that eat their crops.

Foraging OUCH!

You Cannot Sneak Up on Me!

Many spiders and insects, including this sweat bee, look like they are covered in small hairs when you see them under a microscope. These hairs help the animals pick up air vibrations made by nearby predators and prey. The hairs have nerve cells at their ends that send information to the brain.

Protective Parents

Weekend gardeners are rarely glad to see red wasps because the females protect their nests by stinging people who come near them.

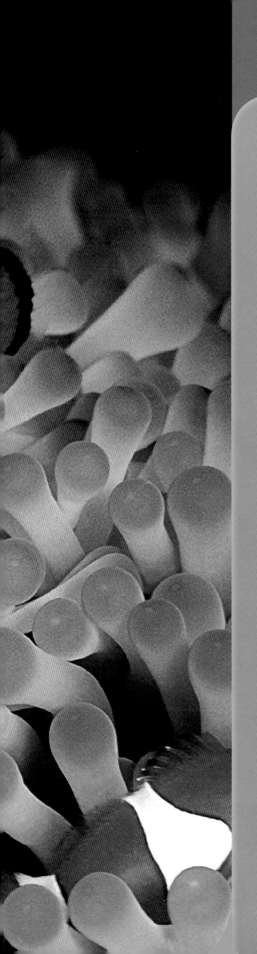

Defense
OUCH!

DEFENSE: the ways organisms protect themselves from predators and their environment

From narwhal swords to stingray tails, animal defenses can make you say OUCH! Animals use amazing behavior and anatomy adaptations to get food and territory, and to protect themselves and their families.

rattlesnake

Venom Ouch

Only about 300 species of snakes have venom, but many of them pack a powerful punch. Rattlesnakes and copperheads have venom called hemotoxins. The enzymes in this type of venom destroy red blood cells. It also causes breathing problems and organ damage. The strength of a snake's venom can vary from place to place, depending on the size of the prey and whether it has developed some resistance to the venom.

copperhead

Defense OUCH!

Toxic Ouch

Poison dart frogs from South America defend themselves with hundreds of toxins in their skin. Until recently, biologists thought these chemicals were a defense against small birds, mammals, and reptiles. New research from the Smithsonian Conservation Biology Institute shows that the frogs need more protection from arthropod predators such as insects and millipedes.

Strong Bites!

Crocodiles and alligators have some of the strongest jaw muscles ever measured. The muscles that close their jaws exert thousands of pounds of biting pressure. The saltwater crocodile in Australia set the record with 3,700 pounds of pressure! Without this type of bite force, crocodiles and alligators would not be able to feed on large prey such as buffalo, antelope, and other mammals.

Safe Harbor

Clownfish secrete special mucus that protects them from anemone stings. The anemones provide the fish with a predator-free habitat, while the clownfish provide the anemones with extra oxygen from their fins.

Crabs and some other crustaceans can feed on anemones because they are immune to the anemone's toxins. Many species have patterns on their exoskeletons that help them hide from predators while they eat.

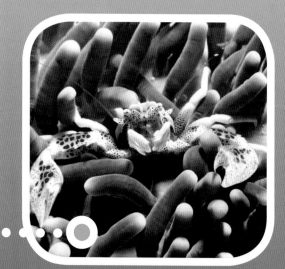

Stinging Cells

One group of animals, called the Cnidarians (ni-dare-e-anz), use special stinging cells to release toxins for protection from predators. Jellyfish, anemones, and corals are in this group.

Cnidarian toxins go unused until the animal receives even the slightest touch, then thread-like coils unravel and deliver hundreds or thousands of stings. Some Cnidarians, such as the box jellyfish in Australia, have toxins strong enough to kill large animals, including people.

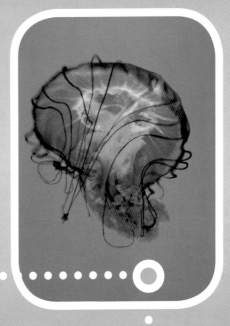

Jellyfish Snacks

Many jellyfish live their lives on the water's surface, floating as part of plankton and feeding on fish eggs and small animals. Other jellyfish, such as the one at left, move through deep waters with more than five feet of stinging tentacles trailing behind.

Safe Pups

Stingrays and great whites give birth to live babies, called pups, instead of laying eggs. Since the moms are well defended from most predators, it is safer for the developing embryos to grow inside their moms than inside of eggs or egg cases that are released into the water.

Venom Tails

Stingrays use their tails for more than just swimming. They also use them for protection from predators such as sharks and other large fish. The end of a stingray's tail has one or more spines on it, and the spines have sharp, serrated edges, like steak knives. When predators get too close, stingrays use their tails like a whip, cutting and stinging their enemies as they move their tails back and forth.

 **Defense** OUCH!

Shark Bait

How much chewing could you do with 300 knife-like teeth? Not much if you were a great white shark. These apex predators use their bottom teeth to hold prey, and their top teeth to tear prey into smaller pieces. Sharks have several rows of teeth and can move new teeth in from back rows when the front teeth fall out.

Bull Fights

Most sea lion species live in large groups called colonies that contain many harems. Each harem has one large male, a bull, a dozen or so females, called cows, and their young offspring. Zebra fights (see page 52) are violent when males defend just a few females. Imagine how brutal sea lion bull fights are when males are protecting dozens of females!

Defense OUCH!

Sword Fights

Also known as sea unicorns and unicorn whales, narwhals live in Arctic seas. Both males and females have two front canine teeth. In females, the teeth do not break through the skin. In males, one tooth grows outward in a spiraling shape, forming 6- to 9-foot-long tusks. Males tusk-fight with other males, and females may use the results of these fights to choose mates. Some males end up with scars and broken tusks from these fights.

Defense OUCH!

Home, Sweet Home

Birds often fight over the best places to build nests. These fights can be very intense, and often determine which birds get to reproduce. Good nesting sites are close to food and have few predators nearby. Good nesting sites also help camouflage eggs and are just the right temperature for growing embryos.

My Nest! No, MY Nest!

Spoonbills, egrets, storks, and herons live in large groups that compete for nest space and nest-building sticks in the trees near rivers, swamps, and ponds. Most fights are settled by verbal threats and chases. Above, a spoonbill (right) confronts a young egret.

Flying High

Eagles put on fabulous shows when males fight for feeding or nesting territories, and during courtship displays. Sometimes, the birds extend and lock their talons. Other times, they do cartwheel-like rolls in the air, pulling up right before they hit the ground.

Stop, Thief!

Jackals live in Africa, Europe, and South Asia. Like many animals, jackals travel far and work hard for their food. When jackals find food, they eat quickly so other animals cannot steal it. After returning to their dens, males and females regurgitate food for their cubs and their mates.

Vultures often steal fresh-caught food from jackals. Other times, jackals do the stealing, sneaking in between a group of feeding vultures for a quick bite before running away.

Defense OUCH!

Badger Fights

Badgers mark their territories with their scent, and they bite and chase trespassers. Why do badgers care so much about where they live? Badgers are strong diggers, and usually have many burrows in their territory. Burrows help badgers escape from predators, and also serve as hiding places for extra food and as protection for cubs.

Badgers defend themselves from large predators with lots of loose skin around their thick, muscular necks. When large carnivores try to attack badgers from behind, they often end up with a mouth full of skin and fur. Badgers can rotate their bodies while in a predator's mouth, then they claw and bite their attackers' faces.

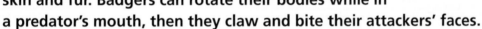

Practice or Play?

Hoary marmots are small North American mammals that live in groups. Young marmots are known for an unusual behavior: they appear to wrestle for hours at a time, standing upright and pushing against each other. Are they learning how to fight? When biologists studied more than 800 marmots, they found that these play fights help decide which animals have higher status in their social groups.

Muzzle Madness

If you were to spend time on any of the large rivers in Africa where hippos live, you would see a lot of hippopotamus fights. Young males fight other young males to learn how to fight; adult males fight other males to decide who is in charge; males and females fight during courtship; and adult females with their calves fight anything that comes near them. What's it like to fight with a hippo? With huge jaws and two pairs of long, sharp tusks, you do not want to find out. Hippos kill more people than crocodiles kill every year.

Defense OUCH!

Tusk Teeth

A hippo's tusks are adaptations in their incisor and canine teeth. Tusks can be 15 to 20 inches long, and sharpen themselves when hippos eat. Thank goodness hippos are vegetarians!

Double Trouble

What's worse than a jaw full of sharp, curved teeth? Two jaws, that's what! Many eels have a second jaw that moves in from the back of their mouths when they feed.

Defense OUCH!

Hang on!

South American sloths use their long, sharp claws to spend almost 24 hours a day hanging upside down in trees, feeding on nearby leaves and fruit. When they come down to urinate (pee) and defecate (poop), their claws serve as defense from predators.

Play Ball!

Pangolins are endangered mammals that live in deep burrows in Asia and Africa. They feed on termites and ants in their mounds with long, thin tongues. Pangolins are covered in thick, overlapping scales made from keratin. When threatened by predators, pangolins roll into a ball. Lions and hyenas cannot get enough jaw traction to chew through pangolins when they are in ball shapes, but biologists have watched lions trying to eat them for hours at a time. OUCH!

bison

bull moose

Crash . . . OUCH!

The American bison (also called a buffalo) is the largest mammal in North America. Both males and females have thick skulls and short, curved horns. To fight, they crash into other bison or predators head first.

The bull moose is the tallest mammal in North America. Males have large antlers that advertise their strength and health to females. Moose antlers are often more than 5 feet wide.

Defense OUCH!

Piercing Canines

Zebras live in small herds with one male, several females, and their young offspring. Male zebras fight when a rival male tries to take over their group of females, called a harem. Zebra fights begin with threats, and then quickly escalate to ferocious biting and kicking. Male zebras have extra-large canine teeth, and often try to bite rivals in the neck, where large carotid arteries bring blood to the brain.

Road Rage

Two chameleons on the same branch is one chameleon too many. These territory transgressions usually don't go well, beginning with hissing and biting threats. Usually, one chameleon leaves before real skin-piercing biting begins.

Environmental OUCH!

ENVIRONMENT: the living (biotic) and nonliving (abiotic) parts of where an organism lives

From frozen ground to super-loud sounds, the rough environments animals live in can make you say OUCH! Animals use some amazing adaptations to make homes, raise offspring, and avoid predators.

Ice Bath

A thick layer of blubber keeps penguins warm when they swim through icy-cold waters, searching for food.

Cold Feet?

How can Antarctic penguins stand on the ground without their warm feet freezing to the ice they are standing on? Penguins and other cold-climate birds have fewer blood vessels in their lower legs, which keeps the temperature in their feet lower than the temperature in the rest of their body. Penguins contract blood vessels in their feet in cold temperatures, and expand them in warmer temperatures. Penguins also huddle together in large groups to stay warm.

Environmental OUCH!

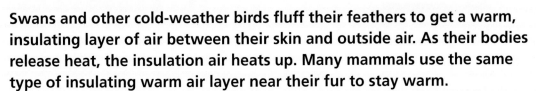

Snow Blankets

Swans and other cold-weather birds fluff their feathers to get a warm, insulating layer of air between their skin and outside air. As their bodies release heat, the insulation air heats up. Many mammals use the same type of insulating warm air layer near their fur to stay warm.

Cold-weather birds can also use snow to keep them warm. Snow? Isn't snow cold? Yes, but sometimes it's warmer than the outside air.

polar bears

Waterproof Fur

Polar bears and sea otters use two layers of fur to stay warm and dry. The outer fur layer is waterproof. The inner fur layer serves as insulation, trapping warm air next to their skin.

These two layers may seem like perfect solutions when you first learn about them. For polar bears, two layers of fur are not enough to live in their Arctic habitat. They also need a fat layer, which they get from eating high-fat meals such as seals.

When global climate change decreases the amount of Arctic ice, a domino effect can happen. When they are hunting for fish, seals use ice as resting spots, and holes in the ice as air holes. Polar bears catch seals by ambushing them when seals are on or near the ice. With less ice, there is less food for polar bears.

Environmental OUCH!

sea otters

Arctic Warmth

Snowy owls hunt for small mammals, birds, and eggs during the day, so they need to be well camouflaged. Their white and light brown feathers help the owls blend in with their environment. Snowy owls have thick insulation feathers to keep them warm.

Ectotherm Energy

Ectotherms such as lizards use heat from the sun to warm their bodies. The more heat they have, the more blood their hearts can pump through their bodies, which helps many types of cells make more energy. Ectotherms can survive at many different body temperatures, but they do everything faster and better when their body temperatures are higher.

agama lizard

collared lizard

Hot Rock Ouch

Rocks hold the sun's heat, even at night. To maximize the amount of heat they get from rocks, lizards flatten their bodies so there is more body surface that can absorb heat. When their body temperatures get high enough, lizards lift part or all of their bodies off the ground so they will absorb less heat.

Environmental OUCH!

Spike Fights

Marine iguanas live in the Galapagos Islands in South America. They feed on algae up to 75 feet under the cool Pacific Ocean waters. When they aren't feeding, marine iguanas leave the water to avoid aquatic predators, and to sun themselves on warm lava rocks. The spikes running down the heads and backs of male marine iguanas may help to protect males when they butt heads during fights.

Step by Step on Special Feet

Watching a mountain goat walk across rocky, high-elevation mountain passes can make you hold your breath. HOW do they do it? Amazing feet, that's how! Goat toes are protected on the edges by toenail-like hooves that latch on to small cracks in the rocks. The pads on their toes are not smooth, like cat and dog pads, which give them traction and keeps them from slipping. Why would an animal live on rocky cliffs? To avoid meat-eating predators such as wolves and mountain lions, that's why!

Environmental OUCH!

Suction Cup Feet

Have you ever watched a squirrel climb down a tree? Unlike most animals that carefully scoot down, feet first, squirrels can run down a tree head first. They can also hang upside down, which helps them gather nuts and steal birdseed from squirrel-proof bird feeders. The secret? An adaptation in their ankle joints that lets squirrels rotate their feet 180 degrees. Squirrels also have long, strong, super-sharp claws.

Check out the back feet of this squirrel. Notice how its toes are spread apart? Spreading their toes this way gives them more surface area to hang on with and more traction.

Spiny Nest OUCH!

Some birds build their nests in cactus plants to protect their young from predators. Birds have scales on their feet, which protect them from sharp spines.

woodpeckers

Marking Your Territory

Howler monkeys live in South and Central America. Males make loud, ear-piercing calls from trees high above the ground. Males call at the same time as other members of their troop, and the loudness and locations of these calls tells other troops where territory boundaries are. Territories are worth defining and protecting for howler monkeys because they contain important foods such as fruit and foliage.

Environmental OUCH!

Laughing Your Life Away

Foxes and hyenas use many sounds to communicate with each other. When they meet an animal with a higher social rank, they make laughing sounds to avoid a fight.

Look at Me!

Like many animals, male moose call to females with a range of songs. Some songs are like barks, while others sound like croaks or deep roars. These sounds also tell other males to stay out of their territory.

Drumming for Attention

Male frigate birds from South America can inflate their red throat pouches like balloons. When they make certain beak movements, it makes drum-like sounds that attract females.

Environmental OUCH!

What a Headache . . .

Woodpeckers use sharp, strong beaks and strong neck muscles to drill holes into trees filled with protein-rich insects. Spongy, plate-like bones help absorb the shock and prevent damage to their brains. Woodpeckers also have an adaptation in their throat bones called the hyoid: the bone wraps up and around their skulls, helping to absorb more shocks.

prairie dog

Look at Me!

Several types of group-living mammals make alarm calls to warn family members and neighbors about nearby predators. Biologists who study prairie dog alarm calls have found that small differences in the calls reveal the type of predator.

Environmental OUCH!

Back Scratching? Maybe Not . . .

What happened when biologists posted trail cameras at bear scratching sites? They found out that bears return to the same trees to scratch year after year. They also learned that males scratch much more than females, and that some males scratch several times a day. All of this back rubbing may not be about itches, though. Bears may be leaving chemical messages for other bears when they scratch. These messages share information about the bears' sizes, territories, and genetic relationships.

Nap Time

Animals choose their sleep spots for their closeness to food and their protection from predators. Here, both a kangaroo and its joey enjoy a sweet sleep.

Belly Flops

Like other whales, humpbacks breathe with lungs, not gills, so they come to the surface for air. Marine biologists have named many of the moves whales make on the surface, including the roll, the side fluke, the tail arch, jaw clapping, head slapping, flippering, breaching, and half breaching (also called a belly flop). Humpbacks use these behaviors to show dominance to other humpbacks, as part of courtship, and as skill-learning play.

Environmental OUCH!

Lounge Chairs?

Sitting on flower spines or iguana horns might spell O-U-C-H for you or me, but for amphibians and reptiles, these perches provide protection without pain. Amphibian and reptile skin is porous, allowing oxygen and carbon dioxide to diffuse in and out. Their skin is also very strong, serving them well in rough habitats.

Nightmare on Ecosystem Street

Some species thrive when they enter a new ecosystem. Their new homes may not have the predators that keep their population numbers in check, and they may be able to out-compete native species for food and habitat. These invasive species (also called alien species) can do a lot of physical damage to an environment, and they can also drive many native species to extinction.

Lionfish are an example of an invasive species that has done a lot of damage to ecosystems. Lionfish are found naturally in Indonesia, and their venomous

spines are well adapted for the predators in their original homes. Lionfish are now found along Atlantic coastlines in North America and in some Caribbean waters. People who keep fish as pets have released them into oceans. Since female lionfish can lay about a million eggs twice per year, the damage to these marine ecosystems is painful to imagine.

Environmental OUCH!

Alien Snakes

Without natural predators, it did not take long for a few Burmese pythons to reproduce enough to become the top predator in the Florida Everglades. The pythons feed on native bobcats, opossums, raccoons, alligators, rabbits, and more.

Good Intentions, Bad Results . . .

In the 1930s, people brought some nutria animals from South America to the United States. Also called coypu and river rats, these large rodents can weigh more than 20 pounds. People thought the nutria would provide work for fur farmers, and for a while there were more than 600 nutria farms.

When nutria farming didn't work well, some farmers released their animals into the wild. Without natural predators, nutria populations reproduced rapidly. Decades later, millions of nutria damaged many river and marsh ecosystems by changing the environment with their plant feeding and den digging. Today, nutria numbers have gone down because of work done by the U.S. Fish and Wildlife Service to remove them.

SCAVENGER HUNT CHALLENGES

Porcupines use their quills for protection from predators. The quills are made from a protein called keratin. **SCAVENGER HUNT CHALLENGES:** Inside, do an image search for "porcupine quill magnified." Do a separate search for "human hair magnified." How different do the two images look? Outside, find a sample of some form of keratin-based protection: a feather? a scale? something else?

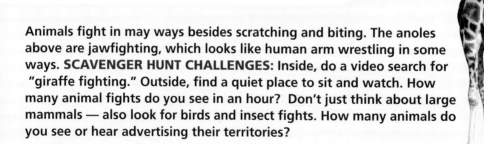

Animals fight in may ways besides scratching and biting. The anoles above are jawfighting, which looks like human arm wrestling in some ways. **SCAVENGER HUNT CHALLENGES:** Inside, do a video search for "giraffe fighting." Outside, find a quiet place to sit and watch. How many animal fights do you see in an hour? Don't just think about large mammals — also look for birds and insect fights. How many animals do you see or hear advertising their territories?

Arthropods such as crabs, scorpions, spiders and insects have exoskeletons that protect them from the environment and from predators. Exoskeletons pose a problem, though, when young arthropods grow because exoskeletons cannot grow with the animal inside them. Instead, arthropods molt when they have grown too large for their exoskeletons, leaving the old exoskeleton behind. **SCAVENGER HUNT CHALLENGES:** Inside, do an image search for "arthropods and molting." Outside, find several abandoned exoskeletons.

Tusks make good defense tools for animals to protect their territories, their mates, and their young. **SCAVENGER HUNT CHALLENGES:** How many animals can you name that have tusks? Can you think of any female animals with tusks?

READ MORE

AFTER THE KILL written by Darrin Lunde and illustrated by Catherine Stock; Charlesbridge (2011).

ANIMALS THAT MAKE ME SAY WOW! by Dawn Cusick; Imagine/Charlesbridge (2014).

THE POLAR BEAR SCIENTISTS by Peter Lourie; Houghton Mifflin (2012).

A WARMER WORLD by Caroline Arnold; Charlesbridge (2012).

FROM THE NATIONAL WILDLIFE FEDERATION:

Fun on the web:
http://www.nwf.org/Kids/Games.aspx for a world of kids' fun

Magazines: RANGER RICK and RANGER RICK JR.

Adaptation: A change in an organism's behavior or form that helps it compete better.

Behavior: The ways organisms act.

Carnivore: An animal that eats other animals.

Communication: The sharing of information. Some organisms communicate with sounds or movements, while others communicate with colors or chemicals.

Diffusion: The movement of gasses or liquids from places of higher concentration to places of lower concentration.

Ecosystem: The living and nonliving parts of an environment functioning together.

Habitat: The home for an organism or a group of organisms.

Hatchling: An animal that has recently hatched from an egg.

Herbivore: An animal that eat plants.

Keratin: A type of protein that makes up beaks, feathers, scales, claws, fur, hair, and more.

Larva/Larvae (singular/plural): The worm-like, wingless stage of some types of newly hatched insects.

Parasite: An organism that uses other organisms for food and habitat.

Plankton: The group of living and non-living things that float on the surface of large bodies of water. Plankton is the foundation of the world's food chain, and contains a lot of eggs, seeds, and algae.

Predator: An organism that preys on other organisms.

Prey: An animal being hunted or eaten by another animal.

Regurgitate: To vomit partially digested food.

Solitary: Living or acting alone.

Territory: An area that an organism lives in and defends.

Toxin: A poisonous substance produced by organisms to help defend themselves from predators or to help them kill prey.

Venom: Poison used by an organism as part of its defense or to find food that is moved through a bite or a sting.

RESEARCH

The author would like to thank and acknowledge the following scientists, organizations, and institutions for their research assistance.

Alaska Department of Fish and Game, Paul T. Andreadis, Animal Diversity (University of Michigan), Arizona State University School of Life Sciences, Arctic Studies Center/National Museum of Natural History, Australia Zoo, BBC Nature, John L. Behler, Biomimicry Education Network, Daniel T. Blumstein, Herber T. Boschung, Gary Brown, John Bull, David K. Caldwell, Melba C. Caldwell, Shirley Casey, The Center for Conservation Biology, Douglas Chadwick, Lawrance K. Chung, Cornell Lab of Ornithology, T. Dabelsteen, James D. Darling, Davidson College, Michael E. Dorcas, Terry Dunn, Theo Emery, Greg Erickson, Evan Eskew, R. D. Estes, John Farrand, Beth Fielding, Florida Fish and Wildlife Conservation Commission, Galapagos Conservation Trust, Crystal Gammon, Brian Giddings, Daniel W. Gotshall, Greenland Institute of Natural Resources, Guy Harvey Ocean Foundation, Randy Hanzal, Steve Harris, Kristen M. Hart, Samantha Hauserman, Hawaiian Islands Humpback Whale National Marine Sanctuary, M. E. Heath, Mads Peter Heide-Jørgensen, D. F. Hoffmeister, hyaenidae.org, Hydrozoan Society, Idaho Public Television, Robin J. Innes, International Shark Attack File (University of Florida), Corinne Kendall,Craig Knickle, Doug Larsen, R. Lewison, N. Lim, Gary H. Lincoff, Edward L. Little, V. Madsen, MarineBio.org, Carol Martins, Melissa Mayntz, V. Mazak, Frank J. Mazzotti, Rita Mehta, Walter E. Meshaka, Michigan Department of Natural Resources, Melissa A. Miller, Lorus Milne, Margery Milne, Minnesota Department of Natural Resources, Monterey Bay Aquarium, Mote Marine Laboratory, Darren Nash, National Oceanic and Atmospheric Administration, National Museum of Natural History (Department of Systematic Biology), National Park Service, National Wildlife Federation, Angela Neal, New Hampshire Public Television, P. K. L. Ng, William A. Niering, Ronald Nowak, Ohio State University Extension, W. Oliver, Nancy C. Olmstead, Oregon Zoo, D. Osorno, J. L. Osorno, Owen Nevin, C. Packer, Jason Palmer, A. E. Pusey, Robert Michael Pyle, Raptor Research Foundation, Robert N. Reed, Reptilis, Michael R. Rochford, Christina M. Romagosa, D. A. Saunders, G. B. SavePangolins.org, Schaller, D. Scheel, Scott Shalaway, C.N. Slobodchikoff, Jennifer E. Smith, Smithsonian Conservation Biology Institute, Smithsonian Zoological Park, Ray W. Snow, State University of New York College of Environmental Science and Forestry, M. F. Sunquist, Texas A&M, Agrilife Extension, Texas Parks and Recreation, J. Scott Turner, University of California-Berkeley, University of Florida Entomology Department, University of Michigan Museum of Zoology, University of Wisconsin-Milwaukee Field Station, U.S. Department of Agriculture, U.S. National Library of Medicine, Jean-Louis Vincent, Vultures Rock, Washington Department of Fish and Wildlife, Paul Weldon, Whale and Dolphin Conservation Organization (WDC), John O. Whitaker, Martin Wikelski, Wildlife Rehabilitators of North Carolina, WildlifeAlliance.org, James D. Williams, John D. Willson, Riley Woodford, World Animal Foundation, World Conservation Union, World Health Organization, Kate Youngdhal, Daniel Zitterbart, and Zoo Atlanta.

INDEX